ANIMAL FRIENDS

ALPHABET BOOK

WRITTEN BY HANNA BRADY & ILLUSTRATED BY JENNY SLIFE

For the marvelous Miss Bins
- Hanna -

&

For all of those who told me to
"make it a book"
- Jenny -

A

is for Alligator

who swims rivers with ease

B

is for Bear

who loves
honey bees

C

is for Chameleon
who plays
hide and seek

D

is for Dragon
who is too big
to sneak

E

is for Elephant
with her
trumpeting call

F

is for Fox
with her
quiet footfall

G

is for Giraffe
who can reach
up so high

H

is for Hedgehog
who is
very shy

I

is for Iguana
who lives in
the trees

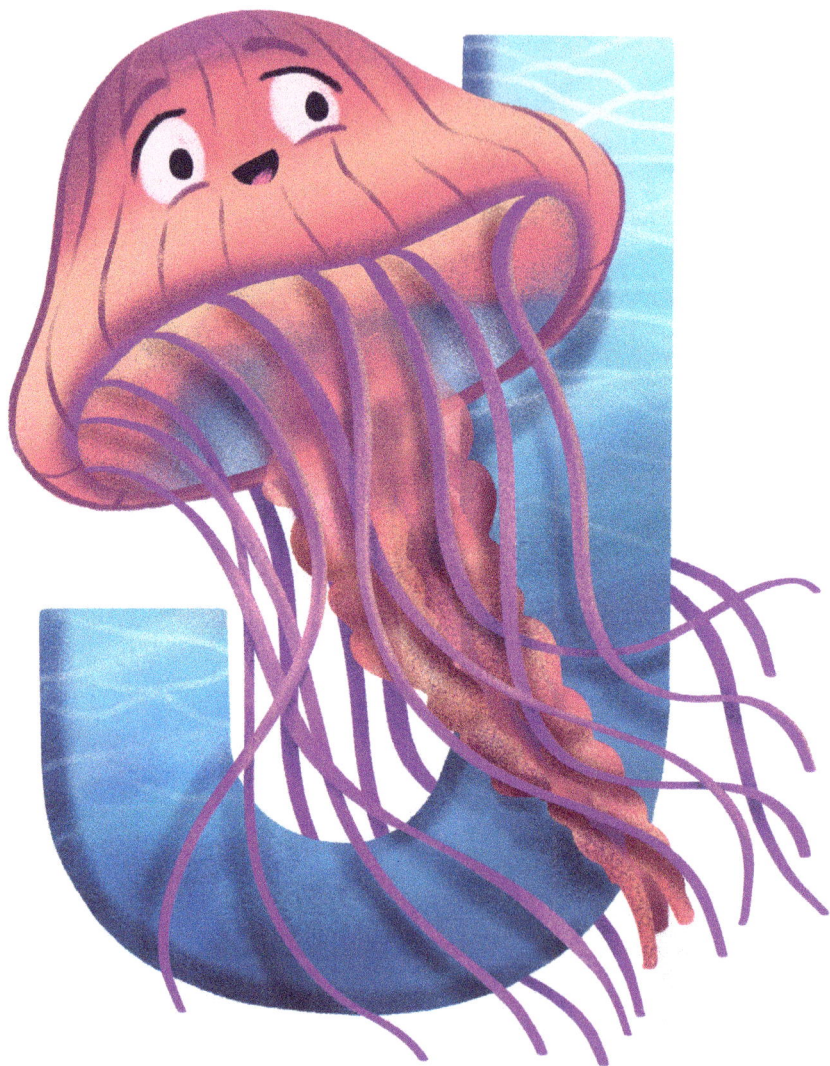

J

is for Jellyfish
who floats through the seas

K

is for Koala
whose hug
is so tight

L

is for Llama
who spits
but won't bite

M

is for Monkey

who swings
vine to vine

N

is for Narwhal

whose horn
is so fine

O

is for Owl
who stays up
quite late

P

is for Penguin
who loves to
ice skate

Q

is for Quail
who is gentle
and shrewd

R

is for Raccoon
who tries
every food

S

is for Sloth
who sleeps
through the day

T

is for Tiger

who pounces and plays

U

is for Unicorn

who makes rainbows for fun

V

is for Viper

who stays warm in the sun

W

is for Walrus
with his tusks
one and two

X

is for X-Ray Fish
who you can
see through

Y

is for Yak
who loves mountains and snow

Z

is for Zebra
with stripes
head to toe

Now we've practiced our letters and found twenty-six friends. Let's go back to A now and do it again!